DANGER DOWN UNDER

BLUE-RINGED OCTOPUS

by Rachel Rose

BEARPORT PUBLISHING

Minneapolis, Minnesota

Credits
Cover and title page, © Subaqueosshutterbug/iStock and © Natalya Bosyak/iStock; 4–5, © SeaTops/Alamy; 6–7, © Michael Patrick O'Neill/Blue Planet Archive; 9, © THIERRY EIDENWEIL/iStock; 10, © AdrianNunez/Shutterstock; 10–11, © ullstein bild /Getty Images; 12, © jungledivers/Shutterstock; 13, © THIERRY EIDENWEIL/iStock; 14–15, © dsi/iStock; 16–17, © John Lewis/Minden; 18, © John C. Lewis/Blue Planet Archive; 19, © John C. Lewis/Blue Planet Archive; 20–21, © Nature Picture Library/Alamy; 22, © MICHAEL WORKMAN/iStock; 23, © Stocktrek Images, Inc./Alamy.

Bearport Publishing Company Product Development Team
President: Jen Jenson; Director of Product Development: Spencer Brinker; Managing Editor: Allison Juda; Associate Editor: Naomi Reich; Associate Editor: Tiana Tran; Art Director: Colin O'Dea; Designer: Elena Klinkner; Designer: Kayla Eggert; Product Development Assistant: Owen Hamlin

Library of Congress Cataloging-in-Publication Data

Names: Rose, Rachel, 1968- author.
Title: Blue-ringed octopus / by Rachel Rose.
Description: Minneapolis, Minnesota : Bearport Publishing Company, [2024] | Series: Danger down under | Includes bibliographical references and index.
Identifiers: LCCN 2023030976 (print) | LCCN 2023030977 (ebook) | ISBN 9798889164999 (hardcover) | ISBN 9798889165064 (paperback) | ISBN 9798889165125 (ebook)
Subjects: LCSH: Blue-ringed octopuses--Juvenile literature.
Classification: LCC QL430.3.O2 R67 2024 (print) | LCC QL430.3.O2 (ebook) | DDC 594/.56--dc23/eng/20230713
LC record available at https://lccn.loc.gov/2023030976
LC ebook record available at https://lccn.loc.gov/2023030977

For more information, write to Bearport Publishing, 5357 Penn Avenue South, Minneapolis, MN 55419.

CONTENTS

DINNER IS SERVED

There's danger Down Under!

With a sudden burst of speed, a tiny creature near Australia's coast grabs a crab in its long, yellow arms. The blue-ringed octopus bites through the crab's shell with a pointy **beak**. Deadly **venom** spreads, and the crab is made into a meal.

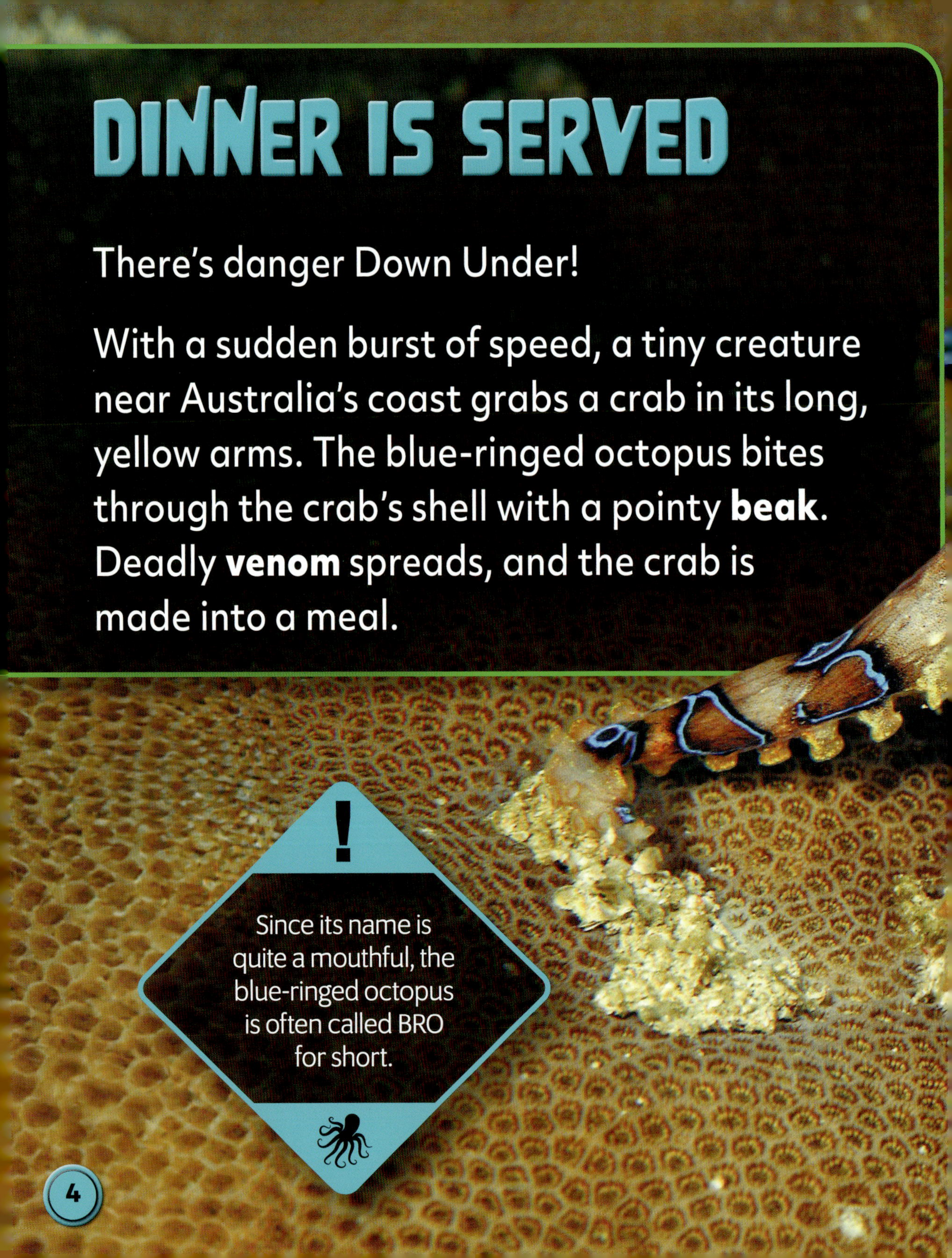

Since its name is quite a mouthful, the blue-ringed octopus is often called BRO for short.

GOLF-BALL SMALL

For an animal with such a big name, the blue-ringed octopus is pretty small. It's only about the size of a golf ball! Like all octopuses, the little BRO has eight arms. In the center of its body where those sucker-covered arms meet is its sharp, birdlike beak. This is the only hard part of an octopus's soft body.

!

Each of the BRO's arms is less than 3 inches (7 cm) long.

WHERE THE BROS GO

There are about 10 different kinds of blue-ringed octopuses scattered across the Indian and Pacific Oceans. Many are found in the warm coastal waters around Australia. They live in **coral reefs** and beachside tide pools. The BROs make sheltered homes under rocks and inside shells.

Like many octopuses, BROs can change color to blend in with their surroundings.

CODE BLUE: STAY AWAY!

Just as its name suggests, the tiny octopus has about 60 blue rings all over its body. When it feels threatened, it lights up these rings. The glowing circles warn **predators** that the BRO is dangerous, so it's best to stay away! If the hungry animals don't heed the bright warning, the octopus will defend itself with a venomous bite.

A MORAY EEL

!

Some animals, such as moray eels and seabirds, eat BROs. They must do so with a surprise attack to avoid the octopus's deadly bite.

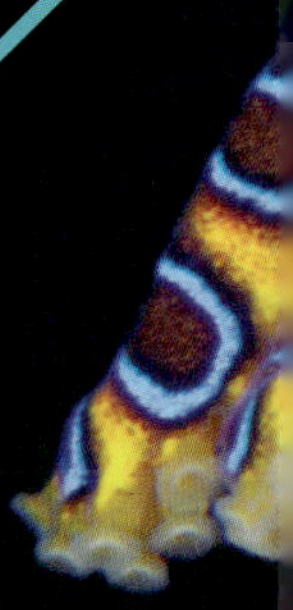

DEADLY WAYS

Deadly venom comes in handy when BROs are hunting, too. These octopuses use their beaks to bite and inject their **prey** with venom. Once the venom has **paralyzed** their prey, the BROs chomp away.

!

BROs eat small creatures with shells, such as shrimp and hermit crabs.

CUTE BUT DEADLY

BRO venom can be deadly for people, too. These eight-armed creatures don't seek out humans, but they will bite if they feel threatened. A person who touches a BRO may not even feel a bite, but the venom acts fast. Soon, the victim will feel weak, have trouble moving, and may have a hard time breathing. They could die unless they get help fast. If you ever see a tiny, glowing octopus, stay away!

Some Australian beaches have signs warning people that blue-ringed octopuses might live there.

TENDER TIMES

Most of the time, blue-ringed octopuses live alone. But BROs do look for each other when it's time to **mate**. The **male** wins over a **female** by gently stroking her with one of his arms. After mating, the female lays up to 100 eggs. She then carries them with her under her arms.

The male BRO dies soon after mating.

A mother BRO
carrying her eggs

SAFETY FIRST

The mother octopus's main goal is to keep her eggs safe. She squeezes into her sheltered home and doesn't leave—not even to hunt for food. After several months, the eggs are ready to **hatch**. But by this time, the mother is so weak from not eating she dies shortly after the babies are born.

!

Blue-ringed octopuses don't usually live past the age of two.

Sometimes, mother BROs turn themselves inside out to protect their eggs.

ARMED AND READY

Baby BROs are about the size of a pea when they are born. The little octopuses eat pieces of crabs or other food scraps they find on the ocean floor. After a month, the young blue-ringed octopuses are big enough to go hunting with their deadly venom. Watch out for this danger in the waters Down Under!

!

Within about a year, BROs are old enough to mate.

MORE ABOUT BLUE-RINGED OCTOPUSES

- BROs have enough toxins to kill up to 26 people within minutes.
- The toxins found in BROs are the same as those in some other creatures, including puffer fish.
- There are about 10 kinds of blue-ringed octopuses, but only 4 have been given names.
- Their beaks are so strong they can bite through a wetsuit.
- Like all octopuses, BROs have three hearts and blue blood!
- Unlike many other octopuses, adult BROs don't have the ability to squirt ink.

GLOSSARY

beak the hard, pointy mouthpart of an octopus

coral reefs underwater structures made from the bodies of animals called polyps

female a blue-ringed octopus that can lay eggs

hatch to come out of an egg

male a blue-ringed octopus that cannot lay eggs

mate to come together to have young

paralyzed made unable to move

predators animals that hunt and eat other animals

prey animals that are hunted and eaten by other animals

venom a dangerous substance that is injected into other animals through a bite

Index

Read More

Buckley, James Jr. *Small but Deadly! Blue-Ringed Octopus Attack (Danger Below!).* Minneapolis: Bearport Publishing Company, 2021.

Levy, Janey. *Black Mamba vs. Blue-Ringed Octopus (Bizarre Beast Battles).* New York: Gareth Stevens Publishing, 2022.

Learn More Online

1. Go to **www.factsurfer.com** or scan the QR code below.
2. Enter "**Blue-Ringed Octopus**" into the search box.
3. Click on the cover of this book to see a list of websites.

About the Author

Rachel Rose writes books for kids and teaches yoga. Her favorite animal of all is her dog, Sandy.